DOODLING

for

ACADEMICS

A Coloring and Activity Book

text by

JULIE SCHUMACHER

illustrations by

LAUREN NASSEF

THE UNIVERSITY OF CHICAGO PRESS

CHICAGO AND LONDON

THE UNIVERSITY OF CHICAGO PRESS, CHICAGO 60637
THE UNIVERSITY OF CHICAGO PRESS, LTD., LONDON

PUBLISHED 2017
PRINTED IN THE UNITED STATES OF AMERICA

26 25 24 23 22 21 20 19 18 17   1 2 3 4 5

ISBN-13: 978-0-226-467047

∞ THIS PAPER MEETS THE REQUIREMENTS OF ANSI/NISO Z39.48-1992
(PERMANENCE OF PAPER).

Acknowledgments

THE AUTHOR WOULD LIKE TO EMBARRASS THE FOLLOWING PEOPLE BY RECOGNIZING THE INFLUENCE OF THEIR WARPED SENSIBILITIES AND TIMELY ASSISTANCE IN REGARD TO THIS PROJECT, NOTING THAT SHE CONSIDERS FAMILY MEMBERS' REMARKS, EVEN WHEN SEEMINGLY UNRELATED, TO BE FAIR GAME: ALLAN AMIS, LISA BANKOFF, LAWRENCE AND EMMA AND ISABELLA JACOBS, KATHRYN MARGE, BARBARA SCHUMACHER, LUCIO TOLENTINO.

THE ILLUSTRATOR WOULD LIKE TO THANK HER HUSBAND ISAAC TOBIN AND BRIDGEPORT COFFEE HYDE PARK FOR NOT KICKING HER OUT THESE PAST MONTHS.

WE THANK MIRANDA MARTIN AT THE UNIVERSITY OF CHICAGO PRESS, RESERVING PARTICULAR GRATITUDE FOR OUR EDITOR, CHRISTIE HENRY, FROM WHOSE 🧠 THIS IDEA ORIGINALLY CAME.

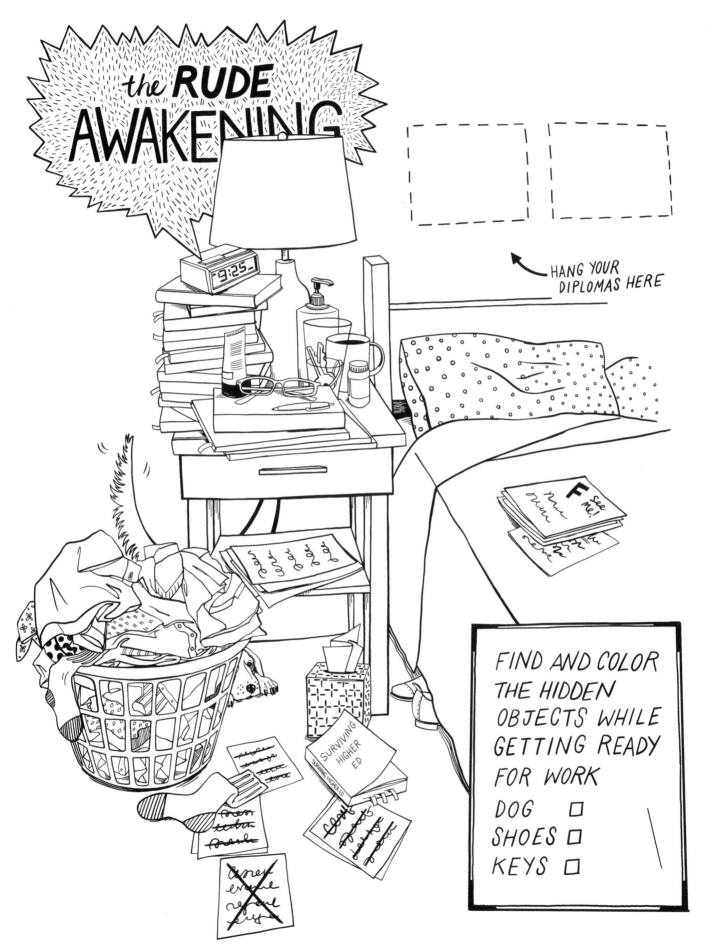

Commuting

MATCH THE MODE OF TRANSPORTATION
TO THE JOB TITLE

ASSISTANT PROFESSOR

PROVOST

STUDENT

ADJUNCT

BOARD MEMBER

NAVIGATION

find the most efficient route through campus

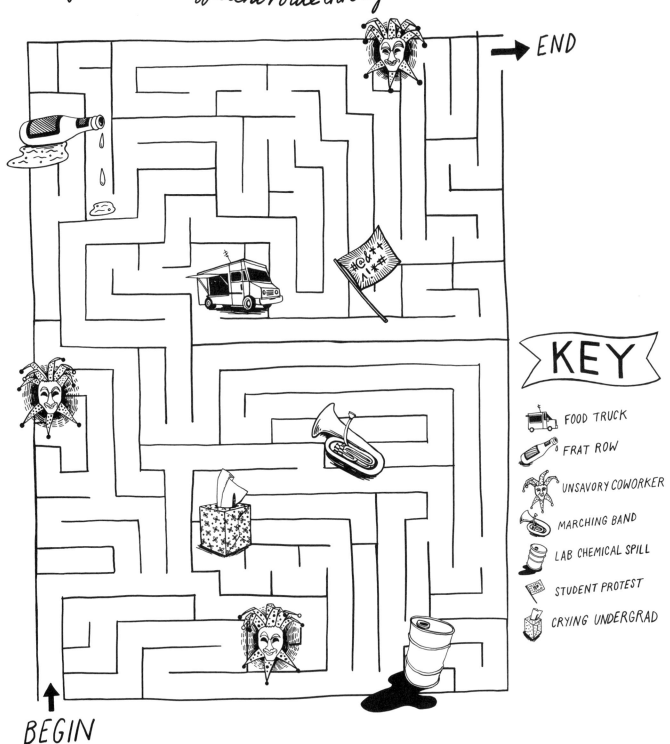

END

KEY

FOOD TRUCK

FRAT ROW

UNSAVORY COWORKER

MARCHING BAND

LAB CHEMICAL SPILL

STUDENT PROTEST

CRYING UNDERGRAD

BEGIN

DEPARTMENT ANNOUNCEMENTS

PIN THE ITEMS TO THE BULLETIN BOARD IN ORDER OF IMPORTANCE

HACKEY SACK CLUB
WEDS 4:30 PM

Maoist Transgender Animal Rights Reading Group Meeting

SWF seeks

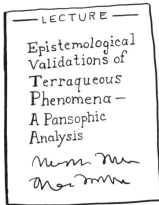

— LECTURE —

Epistemological Validations of Terraqueous Phenomena — A Pansophic Analysis

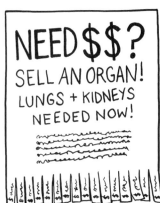

NEED $$?
SELL AN ORGAN!
LUNGS + KIDNEYS NEEDED NOW!

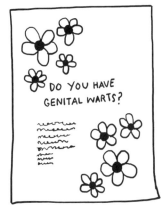

DO YOU HAVE GENITAL WARTS?

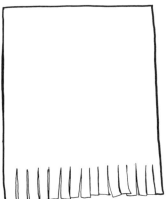

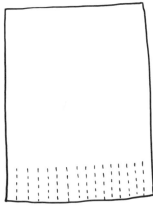

FEEL FREE TO ADD YOUR OWN ANNOUNCEMENTS

Officemate HOBBIES

BAD TAXIDERMY

AMATEUR KOMBUCHA BREWING

WITCHCRAFT ENTHUSIAST

VINTAGE CLOWN MASK COLLECTING

COLOR THE SET THAT BEST MATCHES YOUR OFFICE MATE

ANTACID
VALUE PACK

TARANTULA
PAPERWEIGHT

MINI DOOR
BASKETBALL

CHANGE BOWL

BROKEN
FRENCH PRESS

SLIDE CAROUSEL
COLLECTION

DECEASED PET
PHOTO

EROGONOMIC WRIST PAD

UNWASHED MUGS

REJECTION
LETTERS

tidying up

WHICH OFFICE
OBJECTS
SPARK JOY?

DESK TOY

RUBBERBAND
BALL

DRAFTS

FRUIT FLIES

METAL BOOKEND

JUST-IN-CASE
CARDIGAN

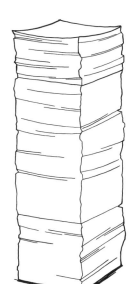
STUDENT PAPERS

GIFT PLANT

DRIED OUT
HIGHTLIGHTERS

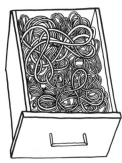
CORD DRAWER

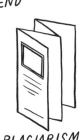
PLAGIARISM
POLICY PAMPHLET

FINANCIAL PRIORITIES

PART ONE

COLOR THE HUMANITIES BUILDING; COLOR THE SCIENCE LAB

THE STUDENT

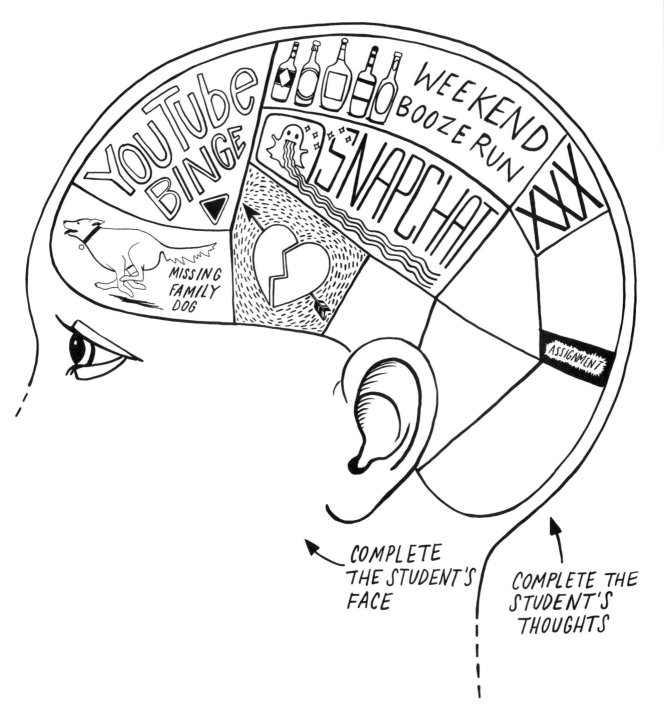

COLOR THE PARTS OF THE BRAIN
THAT ARE FIRING IN THE STUDENT'S MIND

THE FACULTY MEMBER

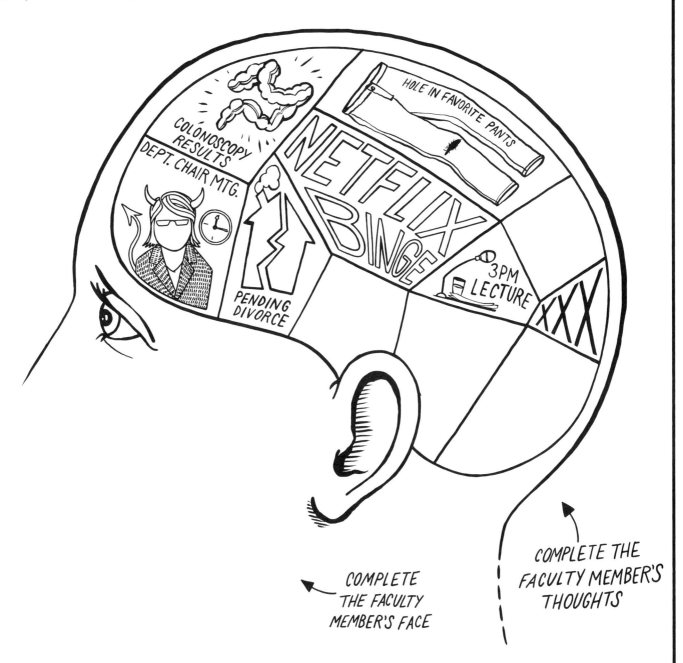

COLOR THE PARTS OF THE BRAIN
THAT ARE FIRING IN THE FACULTY MEMBER'S MIND

FASHION

MATCH THE ACCESSORY TO THE APPROPRIATE CAMPUS PERSONALITY

GRAD STUDENT

DONOR

DEPARTMENT CHAIR

UNDERGRADUATE

COACH

I.T. PERSONNEL

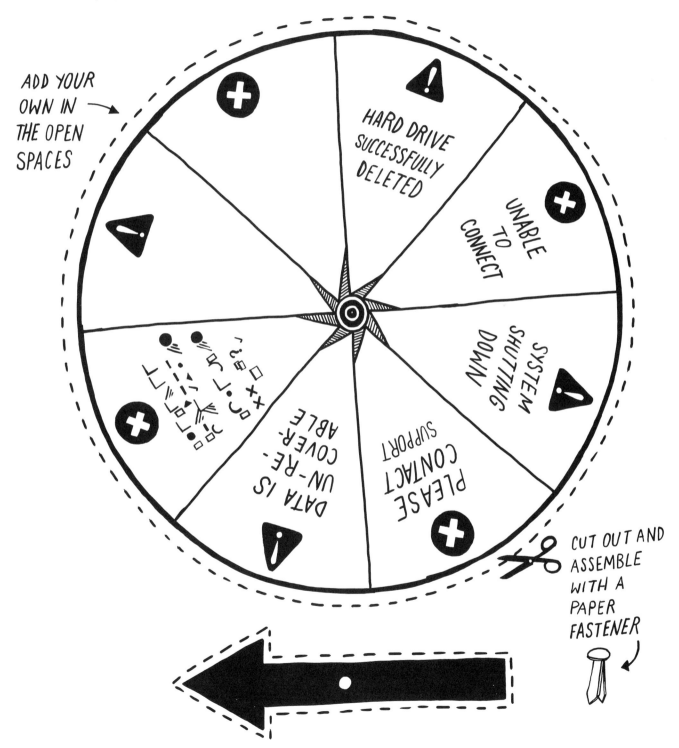

THE COMPETITION

ASSEMBLE A PORTRAIT OF THE SO-CALLED GENIUS WHO WON
THE GRANT YOU APPLIED FOR

CUT OUT FEATURES
AND ACCESSORIES
FROM THE NEXT PAGE
TO CREATE YOUR
GENIUS

HIDDEN PICTURES

FIND AND COLOR THE MANY READERS WHO WILL ENJOY YOUR DISSERTATION

ANGER MANAGEMENT

CIRCLE THE ITEMS TO BE
BROUGHT TO AN APPOINTMENT
WITH THE CAMPUS THERAPIST

↖ -ADD YOUR OWN ITEMS TO BRING HERE ↗

the Creative PROCESS

COLOR THE GRAFFITI IN THE RESTROOM & ADD YOUR OWN TAG TO THE WALL

SCHRÖDINGER'S CAT'S LITTER BOX

full OR empty?

MR. FLUSH

$$\frac{\Sigma x^2 (e^x)/4 + \Sigma F^3 - 31}{\sigma(5y - 15x, p)}$$

professor JONES

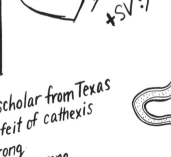

LM + RT
x DC
+ SV : 1

there once was a scholar from Texas
who evinced a surfeit of cathexis
his libido was strong
but his methodology wrong
so he still doesn't quite know what sex is

FRIDGE

CIRCLE THE ITEMS IN THE DEPARTMENT REFRIGERATOR THAT MOST CLOSELY RESEMBLE LUNCH

Student Evaluations of Teaching

REVIEW LAST SEMESTER'S TEACHING EVALUATIONS

PLEASE RATE THE INSTRUCTOR'S EFFECTIVENESS

No comment

PLEASE RATE THE INSTRUCTOR'S EFFECTIVENESS

HORRIbAL

PLEASE EFFE Unt

Never I won't b Don't waste y

PLEASE RATE THE INSTRUCTOR'S EFFECTIVENESS I have called social service and will

PLEASE RATE EFFECTIVENE

HOT!!!
I gave you
on rate my
proffessor.com XXOO

E THE INSTRUCTOR'S
ipper was down
Bad haircut
ad semester

PLEASE R
EFFECTIVEN

o pluto

what I learned in this class

saturn

MARS

PLEASE RATE THE INSTRUCTOR'S EFFECTIVENESS

PEN YOUR DREAM EVALUATION HERE →

ADMINISTRATION

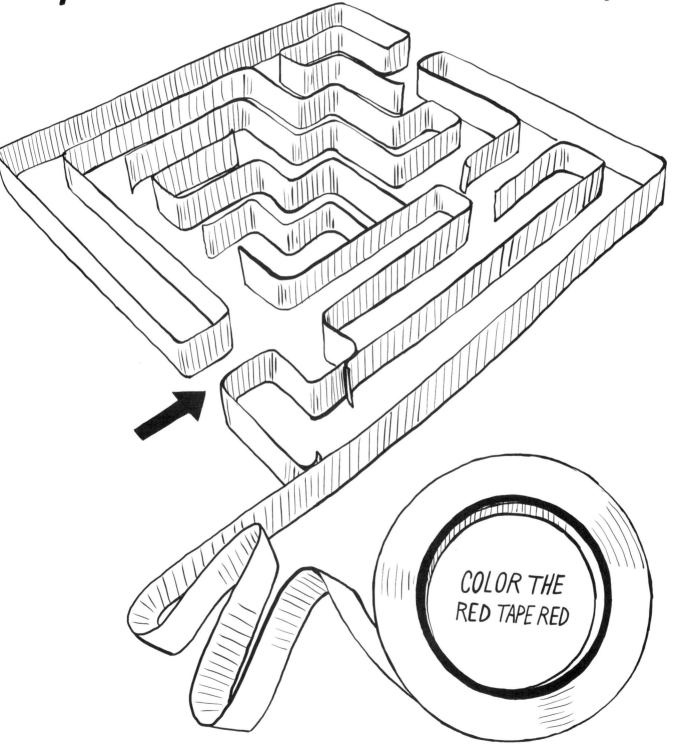

COLOR THE
RED TAPE RED

INTERDISCIPLINARITY

DEVISE A MEANINGFUL PROJECT USING ALL OF THE IMAGES BELOW

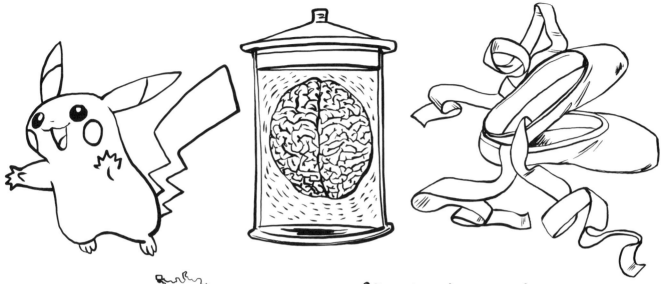

$$\frac{\partial^2 X^{\mu}(\sigma,\tau)}{\partial \tau^2} = c^2 \frac{\partial^2 X^{\mu}(\sigma,\tau)}{\partial \sigma^2}$$

OH AND FEEL FREE TO COLOR AWAY!

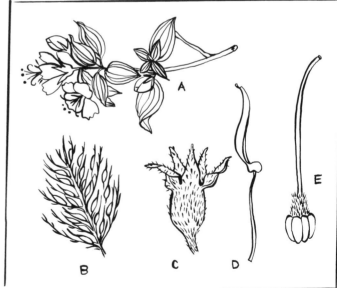

DRAFT YOUR THESIS STATEMENT HERE

OFFICE HOURS

COLOR THE OBJECTS STUDENTS BRING WITH THEM WHEN THEY COME TO YOUR OFFICE

WRONG TEXTBOOK

THERAPY DOG

CLIFFS NOTES ON
CLIFFS NOTES
US $7.49
cliffs NOTES

ADD YOUR OWN OFFICE HOUR PROPS HERE

References

COMPLETE THE LETTER OF RECOMMENDATION

DEAR _____, ①

I UNDERSTAND THAT MY STUDENT HAS
APPLIED TO YOUR _____ ②
FOR THE PURPOSE OF _____. ③
THE STUDENT'S ACCOMPLISHMENTS ARE
_____ ④ AND I AM DELIGHTED
TO RECOMMEND HIM/HER _____
_____ ⑤

WITH ALL BEST WISHES,

_____

1 • PROFESSOR
  • EMPLOYER
  • PAROLE OFFICER
  • WARDEN

2 • GRADUATE SCHOOL
  • SUMMER INTERNSHIP
  • EARLY RELEASE PROGRAM
  • REHAB CENTER

3 • SELF-IMPROVEMENT
  • THEFT/EXTORTION
  • DESTROYING THE
    ORGANIZATION FROM WITHIN

4 • UNIQUE
  • NOT PRINTABLE HERE
  • ONLY OCCASIONALLY ILLEGAL

5 • WITH THE USUAL CAVEATS
  • WITH A CLEAN CONSCIENCE
  • AS LONG AS I NEVER
    HAVE TO SEE HIM/HER
    AGAIN

FINANCIAL PRIORITIES
PART TWO

DRAW 4-6
FIGHTER JETS
IN FLYBY FORMATION

CHOOSE YOUR SEAT

COLOR THE NEW FOOTBALL STADIUM SUBSIDIZED AT THE
EXPENSE OF THE LIBRARY

PROMOTION

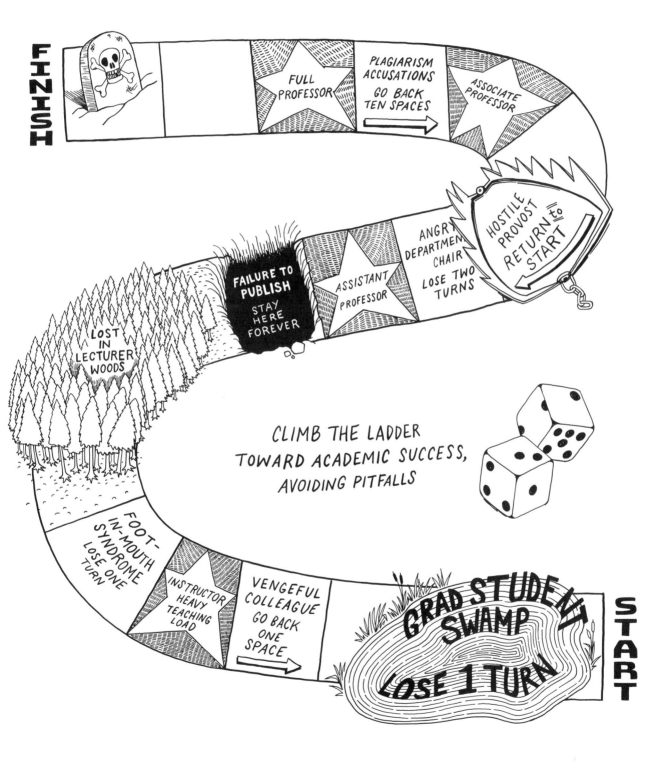

ABSENTEEISM
COLOR AND DECIPHER THE STUDENT'S EXCUSE FOR MISSING CLASS

Assigned Reading

CHOOSE THE TOWER OF BOOKS ASSIGNED TO STUDENTS (COLORING THE BOOKS THAT STUDENTS ACTUALLY READ)

LIST STUDENTS' PREFERRED READING MATERIAL HERE: _____

_____

_____

IN-CLASS EXAM

COLOR THE MOST ORIGINAL
APPROACH TO CHEATING

JUICE BOX
TRAP DOOR

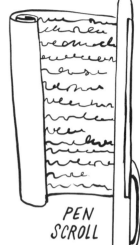

PEN
SCROLL

PROJECTOR
GLASSES

ADD THE MOST
CREATIVE CHEAT
YOU'VE SEEN
HERE →

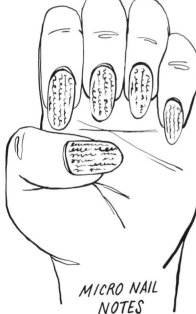

MICRO NAIL
NOTES

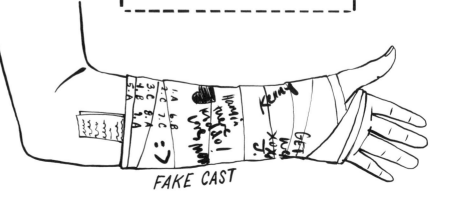

FAKE CAST

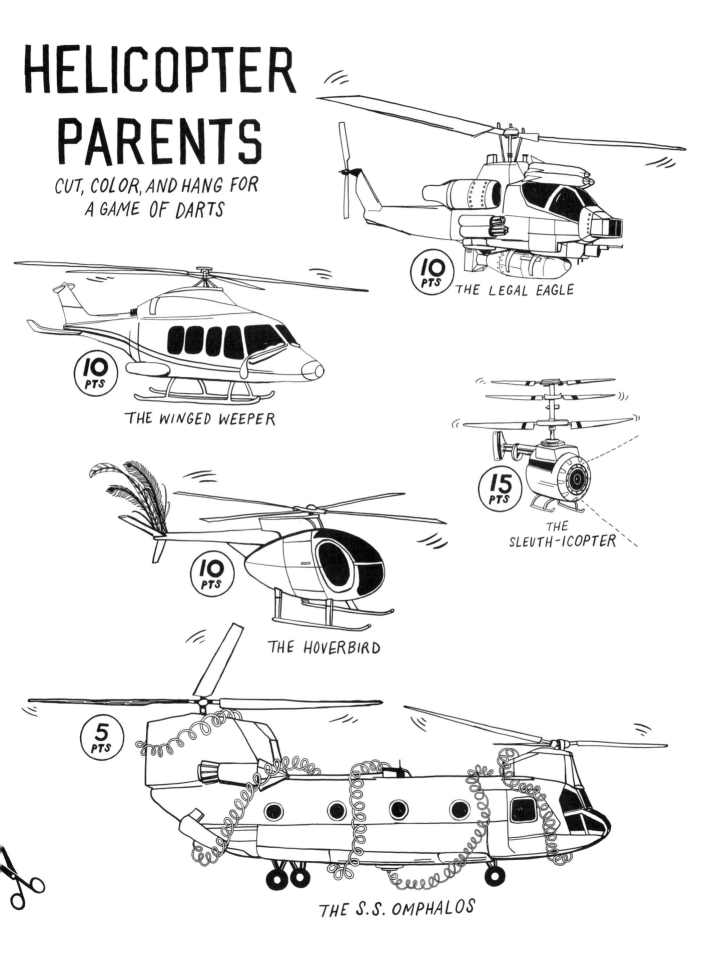

SENSITIVITY

COMPLETE THE TRIGGER WARNING ON THE SYLLABUS VIA THE SELECTIONS ON THE RIGHT

Dear Students,

Please be advised that this _____

includes material that you may find

_____.

Should you require _____,

please contact your _____.

Hoping the semester will leave you

feeling _____,

Professor X

BOOK

FILM

UNIVERSE

UPSETTING

EYE OPENING

CONTRADICTORY TO YOUR WORLDVIEW

MEDICAL ATTENTION

AN ASTROLOGICAL CONSULT

A PERSONALIZED G-RATED CURRICULUM

FILL IN THE BLANK

FAIRY GODMOTHER

LOCAL RED CROSS

READY FOR ADULTHOOD

INTELLECTUALLY INTACT

FILL IN THE BLANK

COLOR THE VENN DIAGRAM FROM THE COMMITTEE MEETING PRESENTATION

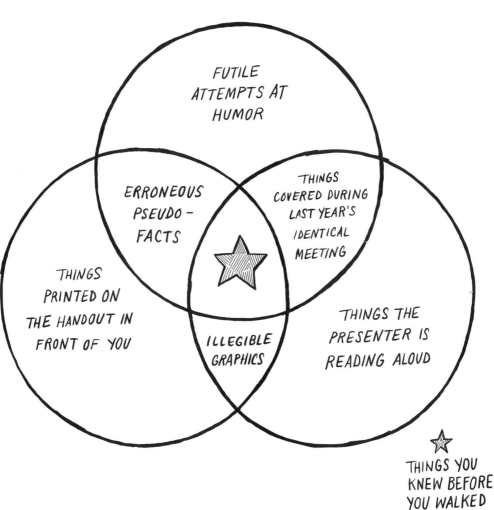

BUILDING THE ACADEMIC BRAND

COLOR THE UNICORN MASCOT OF THE MYTHICAL UNIVERSITY THAT CLAIMS TO BE EXPANDING ITS AMERICAN STUDIES PROGRAM

ADD YOUR OWN OBJECTS TO THROW AT THE UNICORN

ADD YOURSELF HERE FOR A PHOTO-OP WITH THE UNICORN

PUZZLING

complete the word-find during the
visiting scholar's two-hour lecture

E	P	K	S	O	P	H	I	S	T	F	R
O	W	L	O	G	O	R	R	H	E	A	Q
N	B	O	M	B	A	S	T	I	N	L	O
P	J	E	N	N	U	I	A	W	U	L	U
Z	D	R	I	V	E	L	V	K	R	A	M
B	J	P	L	E	B	I	A	N	E	C	B
R	E	G	O	M	A	N	I	A	C	I	V
O	J	A	Q	I	D	O	P	O	M	O	G
W	U	Y	U	F	P	J	B	E	I	U	K
S	N	L	E	T	H	A	R	G	Y	S	E
E	E	D	N	E	U	R	O	S	I	S	P
U	A	B	T	U	R	G	I	D	P	A	U
H	X	V	A	C	U	O	U	S	R	L	J
M	G	R	E	C	O	N	D	I	T	E	Y

1 BOMBAST
2 DRIVEL
3 EGOMANIAC
4 ENNUI
5 FALLACIOUS
6 JARGON
7 JEJUNE
8 LETHARGY
9 LOGORRHEA
10 NEUROSIS
11 PLEBIAN
12 POMO
13 RECONDITE
14 SOMNILOQUENT
15 SOPHIST
16 TENURE
17 TURGID
18 VACUOUS

AFTER HOURS

COLOR ALL THE DRINKS YOU HAD TO PAY FOR
AT THE VISITING SCHOLAR DINNER.
CIRCLE THE DRINKS THAT WERE YOURS.

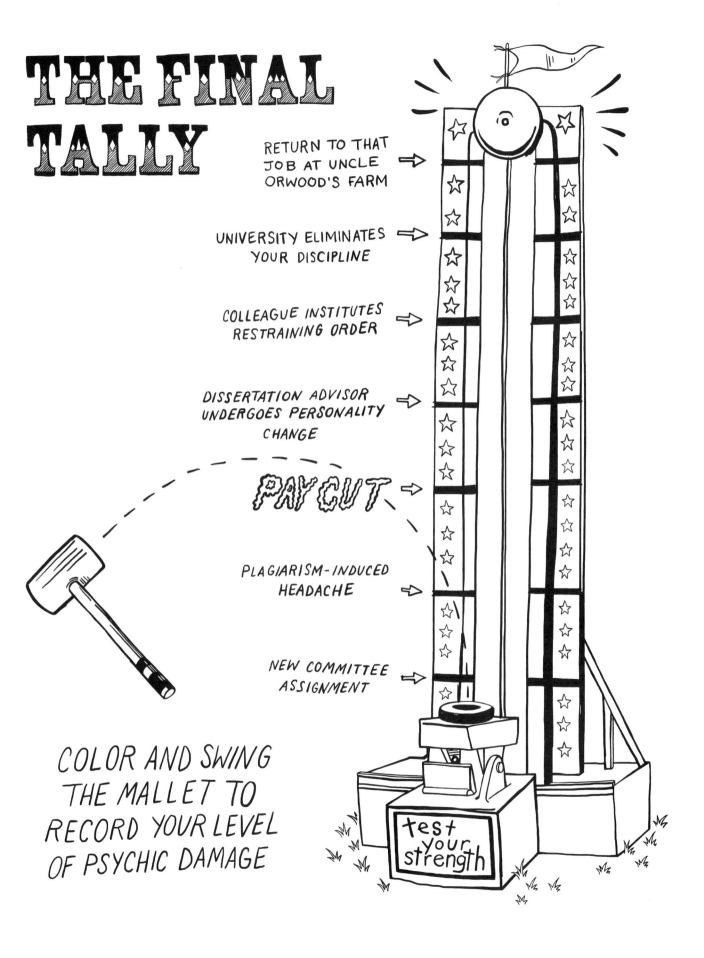